My Blind Wolf

The Evolution of Creation

by

T.G. Maier

authorHOUSE

1663 LIBERTY DRIVE, SUITE 200
BLOOMINGTON, INDIANA 47403
(800) 839-8640
www.authorhouse.com

First published by AuthorHouse 10/14/04

ISBN: 1-4184-2505-2 (sc)

Library of Congress Control Number: 2004093464

Printed in the United States of America
Bloomington, Indiana

This book is printed on acid-free paper.

Grab the tail of

My Blind Wolf.
As she leads you like a pinball
Through the twisted tilt-a-world doors of the mind
On a roller coaster ride into the invisibility that exists beyond
Our reality of time and space
Investigating the metaphoric bond of love between,
Evolution and Creation

A story assembled by
T.G. Maier

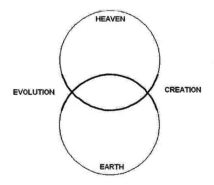

How many of us have taken a look back at the 'tail' of our lives?

"The future is the past healed." – unknown

This book is dedicated to all the Atom and Eves of the world who are searching to reunite with each other and themselves.

"Sometimes a person needs a story more than food to stay alive."
-Ted Andrews – "Animal Speak" (Badger)

Table of Contents

Music List

Here's a list of songs that complement the story. If listened to they may enhance the readers' personal mental visualization and enjoyment of this unique metaphoric adventure:

1. Spirits in The Material World - The Police
2. Great Balls of Fire - Jerry Lee Lewis
3. Stay - Jackson Browne
4. How You Ever Gonna Know - Garth Brooks
5. One Piece at a Time – Johnny Cash
6. Do What You Got to Do - Garth Brooks
7. Living and Living Well - George Strait
8. Wish You Were Here - Pink Floyd
9. Dukes of Hazard Theme - Waylon Jennings
10. The Joker - Steve Miller Band / performed by an animation known as Homer Simpson
11. Sharp Dressed Man - ZZ Top
12. Material Girl - Madonna
13. Come to Poppa - Bob Segar
14. Cold as Ice - Foreigner
15. Tax Man - The Beatles
16. Simple Kind of Man - Lynrd Skynrd
17. Highway to Hell - AC/DC
18. Life's a Dance - John Michael Montgomery
19. Life Without You- Stevie Ray Vaughan
20. Grand Illusion - Styx

Suggestion: If you (the reader) have the opportunity to listen to this list of music, please do so before you read this story. Then as you read your subconscious may be inclined to blend the music with the story.

Introduction

There is a song titled "Spirits in The Material World", by Sting and the Police. Ever think about the *words*[1] in song lyrics?

While waiting for a flight at the Denver airport, I was just hanging out, practicing my skills as an unaccredited behavioral scientist. That's a fancy way to say "people watcher." I felt like I was in a giant waiting room for a 'Star Trek Hollow Deck' program. Each person I observed was experiencing the adventure of his or her own unique individual life program. At these terminals everyone was waiting to board or depart their ride through similar yet different 'star gates'.

We are spirits in a material world. We are living in the coolest virtual reality program ever conceived, just like a 'Star Trck' hologram stage. We are Great actors, who have lost ourselves in the roles we play. It's like we have amnesia, so that we can experience what we are not. We keep running around in circles like a goofy dog chasing its tail, in what we call the Human Race. We have lost focus of our goal or purpose for being, as we compete through the flux of this earth school.

---

[1] Words: Sometimes words have a variety of meanings, and word meanings often change among generations, geographical variations of pronunciation accents, and ethnic based dialects and translations in this evolving multi- lingual eclectic combination of communication modalities of this world we live in. The footnote definitions given in this story only give the meaning(s) that the words have as they are used in the text. Some are current, some are old, some are foreign, and some are combined or created just for the fun of it. If you find any words in this story that you don't know, or have a different meaning based on your life experience, please look them up in good current and antique reference sources, which give information for each word including meaning, pronunciation, etymology, and translations into and from other languages. If you choose not to, then a misunderstanding and possible conflicts may surface.

It is like a scavenger hunt to find our *truth*.[2] We have been distracted for so long, it's time to reconnect and remember what we went shopping for. How did all this get started?

---

[2] Truth: That which is considered to be the supreme reality and to have the ultimate meaning and value of existence. That which agrees with the facts and observations; logical answers resulting from looking over all the facts and data; a conclusion based on evidence uninfluenced by desire, authority or prejudice; an inevitable (unavoidable) fact no matter how arrived at.

What If?...
Door # 1

It's just a little ole love story.

This earth experience began as a Spiritual suburban, high school science project, with all of the students encouraged to participate in the co-creative process.
It became a soul's tale of adventure. It evolved into a spiritual journey through a world wide web of terror; and a race to extinguish the veils of firewalls parroted by earth bound fear mongers, to rediscover what's been missing.

The students were to build a complete new world. Based on the theory of duality, they were instructed to create a dynamic organic bioelectric, interactive, multi-dimensional, holographic learning experience. Just like a holographic multilateral amusement park and becoming a character in your favorite video game.

All of these students already knew the fundamentals of the basic 3-D picture show. They knew that "a hologram is made by sending a single laser beam through an optical devise known as a beam splitter in order to create two laser beams which originate from the same source." [i] 3-D holograms were used every day at the schools as an instructional tool. Holograms permitted the students and teachers the ability to view an image, from various facets as if the image was real. It was very popular with the architecture and design department. They could view a project before it was built. All design conflicts were resolved before the project began. There were no field problems to overcome.

These 3-D programs helped the students unite their understanding of the multifaceted viewing points. Many of the instructors experienced great amusement as the students entered into heated debates, arguing about whose view was right and who was wrong. They were all looking at the same thing. Whenever the hologram was rotated, the students could see what the others were looking at. Opinions and judgments changed as they all began to see the bigger picture. When the kids viewing the object form's from opposite sides stopped ganging up on each other declaring from their point of view that We Are Right (WAR), it was amazing how *industrious*[3] they all became when the balanced collective began to work together towards the common goal. It was like a chorus singing in harmony.

Technology advanced and a new imaging tool was introduced into the schools. This extra-dimensional hologram (4D) was a major step up in the learning curve. This added dimension enhanced the image from a ghost like vision to gave it material / concrete properties. It rearranged all of the 'trons', electrons, neutrons, protons, and produced a specialized energy field known as *matter*[4].

With the introduction of 4-D all who viewed an image could not only see it, they could touch it, feel it, hear it, smell it, taste it, as if it were real. Just like a hollow deck experience.

This multi-dimensional imaging machine, was simply named, the Great Optical Devise. (G.O.D.)
This source is the co-creative entity from which all things manifest into material form.

The teachers supplied the students with the basic parts / elements, energy bands. The kids who were ramroding the project gathered and mixed up the elements in a big kitchen blender type machine. Nothing began to happen. There was no catalyst to get things started. So at the end of this first step in this trial and error process, they just had what looked like a big messy ball of cookie dough.

This ball of stuff needed an influx of energy to get the *reaction*[5] started. They were looking for a source of internal combustion to fuel the perpetual motion of this project.

---

[3] Industrious: Assiduous in work or study; diligent. *Oblolete* Skillful; clever. Applying oneself with energy to study or work; actively and purposefully getting things done; opposite of being idle and accomplishing nothing.
[4] Matter: That of which any physical object is composed; material
[5] Reaction: Reciprocal or return action or influence. Retaliatory or responsive effect of stimulation.

These great minds (kind of nerdy dudes) exchanged ideas in the lab for a while. None of the ideas had the right stuff. After this lab time, they went to gym class where they became targets in their own version of dodge ball.

While they were getting bombarded (as nerds do) they noticed one of their classmates' kind of hiding off to the side with a confident impish grin. This classmate appears to us today in the loveable mischievous image of ArtBay ImpsonSay. (Pig Latin will be used occasionally in this story in hopes to avoid legal b.s.) We'll just call this character Art.

All of a sudden, the top athlete of the school, Sonny (the coach's son) came running out of the locker room, screaming like thunder dancing in a spaztastacular exhibition of rage. The energy that was exuding from this individual can only be described as the type of energy that occurs when matter and antimatter collide annihilating each other…or someone with no concept of rhythm…trying to dance.

Art was rolling on the ground crumpled up in a ball of laughter. He had put an overdose of high strength veterinary liniment in the jocks strap. The cup was definitely…full.

Goodness Gracious "Great balls of Fire!" This was a moment of enlightenment to these great minds! How to power this new world!

One said, Let's use two balls of fire! Another said, naww…we don't need two fireballs. Them two nads just got fused together. We'll power this project with one flaming super ball. We'll name it the son…ya know…got to give the dude his credit. They agreed and our Sun was created.

The coach observed his son's activity. This Coach thought if he could just harness and focus this new energy on the athletic field, they could win a state, maybe even a national championship! (He had known that the kid had great athletic ability, however the child was lazy, did just enough to get by)

It was getting close to lunchtime and they still hadn't figured out how to energize this ball of stuff to get the earth started. While the nerds discussed at their lonely lunch table, Art sat down and listened.

Art spoke up and said, "Hey dudes, just nuke it. That's what I do with my frozen Twinkies when I get the munchies." (Art's Mom would stock up on snacks when they went on sale. She would freeze them so they would last longer. She was a very thrifty Mom with a budget; she had to stretch her dollars.)

Not caught up in an ego battle those at the table mutually agreed to try it. It might just work! They didn't have anything to loose. The worst that could happen was that they might discover another way that didn't work for them.

Immediately they grabbed their ball of earthly elements and stuck them into the cafeteria's microwave oven.
Their attention got sidetracked when 'Sonny' came into the cafeteria. Still burnin' white-hot. He was on a mission to kick Art's ass. Meanwhile, Art was attempting to make his get away without being seen.

When the timer went off they opened the door to the microwave. They had over cooked it. Stuff was spewing out like the cream filling of a Twinkie volcano.

They carefully brought it back to the lab, and dumbfoundedly gawked at it. It was supposed to be an inhabitable interactive world, but at this time it was an extremely hostile environment.

What do we do now? They thought as they scratched their heads. We've got to make this work or we all won't make the grade and graduate.

It was perfect timing when they heard the voice of Art, as he was running down the hall. "Put some water on it Dude! It'll cool off man." Art wasn't talking to them, however he said what they needed to hear! So they poured a bunch of water on this globe of goo and it cooled down.

The oceans had just been created! And a hard crust encapsulated the continually cooking molten mess beneath this superficial shield of delightful water.

4

Now all of the spiritual students who desired to have the experience of fish type bodies in this new material world traveled through the *matrix*[6] of the Great Optical Device, and were beamed into the program. In their new artificial life forms they were able to enjoy the uniqueness of existence swimming around in this great water ball. It was like a big ocean of fun.

Some students just wanted to participate so they could get out of their other classes. The school administration was aware of this, so they placed a time limitation on this new amusement park outing. They called it a Life Time.

All was good.

---

[6] Matrix: The womb. A place or enveloping element within which something originates, takes form, or develops. That which gives form, origin, or foundation to something enclosed or embedded in it, as in a mold for casting. (Webster's New Collegiate Dictionary 1961)

STUNNED
Door # 2

Everyone went home to their families that evening, except for those riding the fish *gig*[7]. The parents asked, "What happened in school today?" The kids actually told them!
This surprisingly stunned many guardians who expected the traditional response… "Nothing."

Many parents went into severe and somewhat incapacitating shock and required medical and psychological counseling! The children had an interest in something at school and they were excited about sharing their experience. It was a dream many parents never thought would ever come true.

The next day, word got out about this exciting world of fun. As the finned ones came back and told stories of their, 'there' experiences, exhilaration of triumph and agony of defeat. More and more of these beings wanted to participate, and enjoy the *practice*[8] of being what ever they chose to BE in this world where there are no victims only volunteers.

However there was an obstacle to overcome. The walking ones, winged ones, standing ones, and the crawling ones, couldn't participate because this world was completely flooded by all the water.

Next challenge, how to get the water level down? As all the great minds gathered and contemplated about it, Art… still running for safety… cut a corner too close and knocked over the drinking water dispenser. A great lake of water covered the floor. It was kind of an eerie sight.

---

[7] Gig: anything that whirls or is whirled; specif., *Obs.*, a top.
[8] Practice: to do or perform (something) repeatedly in order to acquire or polish a skill.

A call was sent out, the janitor; Herby came and cleaned up the mess with a sponge mop.

Meanwhile Cinderella was walking by the doorway of those she considered to be the arrogant academic *aristocracy*[9], and overheard the conversations of their dilemma. She immediately knew the answer: Sponges!!
So Cinderella stuck her head in the door and yelled, "Hey ya'all use Sponges! What's the problem? Yo Mamma's never make you sissies clean up a mess before?" Her stepsisters were among this clique.

Many youthfully energetic beings wanted to try life as a sponge... So by popular demand the sponges were beamed into the world. As the sponges grew, the waters receded. A great island was exposed. It appeared to be a huge turtle shaped island. This super continent was named *Pangaea*.[10]

Now, finally there was no limitation to the forms of participation. However there was one little catch. According to the physics of this *materialistic*[11] *dimension.*[12], participants have to shift their life force frequency band from that of a light being to a frequency string of matter.

News of this experiment traveled at warp speed to all the surrounding neighborhoods of the cosmos. Everyone wanted to participate.

---

[9] Aristocracy: government by a few with special privileges, ranks or positions; rule by an elite few who are above the general law; a group who by birth or position are "superior to everybody else" and who can make or apply laws to others but consider that they themselves are not affected by the laws.

[10] Pangaea: According to the continental drift theory, the supercontinent Pangaea began to break up about 225-200 million years ago, eventually fragmenting into the continents as we know them today. Pangaea, from the Greek, meaning "all islands."

[11] Materialistic / materialism: The theory that physical matter is the only reality and that everything can be explained in terms of matter and physical phenomena; the opinion that only physical matter exists. The theory or attitude that physical well-being and acquiring worldly possessions constitute the greatest good and highest value in life.

[12] Dimension: measure in a single line, as in lineal time.

The 'Nerds' had gotten their revenge. They had created something that the popular crowd wanted to inter-act with. Jellyfish were designed for those with a limp finned swimming style. Anyone could participate. There was no discrimination. The first jellyfish was named Lamar.

The BOREDOM PHENOMENON
Door # 3

Another challenge surfaced. Everyone was getting bored. They all kept doing the same old thing, and the adventures became very predictable. It was time for some upgrades, some changes.

This might have been the time when the concept of free will was being debated?

Young EveStay ArtinMay, one of the biggest dinosaurs, heard a song on the radio from the comedic duo EechChay and OngChay. The song was a classic song, about Santa Claus, and his "magic dust.' Evestay had experienced being a BIG dinosaur, so he took some magic dust and got really small. His body machine changed from a huge dinosaur, to a little lizard.

This was the beginning of the end of the humongous dinosaur era.

An interesting *phenomenon*[13] was occurring in this experiment.

As the polarity of the collective consciousness on the planet grew out of balance, the gyration of the planet changed, it began to spin on a different axis. North became south, and south became north. The sun rose in the west and set in the east. The face of the earth was changing. Mountains were created, kind of like a major pile up on a main highway when someone slams on their brakes during rush hour.

Those who where able to shift their consciousness to a higher level of understanding were allowed to move on to the next phase of the game. Those who held on desperately to the old ways that no longer served their highest good were either eliminated, or, were given another life vehicle and the process of obtaining new understandings and better ways to do things would start over.

---

[13] Phenomenon: an observable fact or event. An unusual, significant, or unaccountable fact or occurrence; a marvel.

Please remember, this was like the 1960's and 70's in the spiritual realms *evolutionary*[14] involvement into various material dimensions. This was a very experimental and colorful time!

The earthly *environment*[15] was very different from the heavenly *realms*[16]. The 'colors' that exist on the home plain are of a frequency band that cannot be detected or seen with the limitations of our human eyes. In order to look into these channels, humans need to use their third eye. Many have forgotten they have one.

Magic dust, became real popular, and kind of a problem during this experimental phase. But real fun! However, some became addicted to this psychedelic experience and forgot what they really were and why they couldn't return home.

In many ways this complex matrix was developing into a prison for the mind. Many outside observers considered it to be an insane asylum. The participants kept repeating the exact same patterns of behavior over and over and over, expecting a different outcome each time. The software of these behavior patterns would be down loaded into the hard drives of future generations by a format known as hereditary inheritance. It was definitely a widespread expansion of multiple parallel realities playing out on single *lineal*[17] dimension time strands. All of this proved to be way too much fun. Ever try to get a child into the car at the end of a vacation, or weekend at the lake? Some just want to "Stay" a little bit longer, play a little bit longer, or go for one more ski ride.

---

[14] Evolutionary: related to a very ancient theory that all plants and animals developed from simpler forms and were shaped by their surroundings rather than planted or created. Evolution: A gradual process in which something changes into a different and usually more complex form. The process of gradual development.

[15] Environment: one's surroundings; the material things around one; the area one lives in; the living things; objects, spaces and forces with which one lives whether close to or far away. The totality of circumstances around an organism or group of organisms, esp.: The combination of external conditions that affect organisms. An Organized Ism ☺! An organized distinctive doctrine, system, or theory.

[16] Realms: A kingdom. Hence, province; region; domain.

[17] Lineal: Of or pert. to a line or lines; linear. Consisting of, or being in, a direct line of ancestry or descendants. Derived from ancestors in the direct line: hereditary.

Sometimes when children are having too much fun they just don't want to go home. And they definitely don't want to help you pack the car.
Take me on one more ride, just one more time… Say you will.

DESEGREGATION?
Door # 4

One of the students who were being bussed to the school wanted to participate in this adventure.

Tommy, and his friends were from the 'man' species. However, like all the other light beings, he lacked what we perceive as color. To enter the program he had to choose a color. To do this he spun a big wheel that had four colors on it. It was a really big wheel just like the one they use today on the game show 'The Price is Right.'

This characters name is Atom. In the physics of this new reality the atom is the smallest unit of matter, yet is a part of something much bigger than its lone self. Atom was the first human. For *aeons*[18] many humans have mispronounced his name as Adam.

Atom was having second thoughts about participating in this adventure known as a life.
His Pop talked with him, and asked some questions to help the young man make his own decision.

He said, "Son, I don't have your answers. But there's a wind whipping out there and it's whistling your tune. It's up to you to chase your dream. The meaning of this thing called life is something that you will have to find out for your self. You will have the opportunity to buy into some cloned prepackaged ideal value meals, which might be cooked up by many who mistake knowledge for wisdom. The cynics will try to find a fall guy to blame for their unhappiness because they are envious of you and have shelved their own dreams. Before you sign on the dotted line… look at the fine print, the itineraries may be different than what they told you they sold you. Troubles will come and they will pass. Follow your heart and nothing else. It's OK to use the menus but ya might want to get your parts a la carte.

---

[18] Aeon: (eon) An immeasurably or indefinitely long period of time.

Your life will not be yours until you assemble it yourself. Custom build it one piece at a time... This will be a real good learning opportunity for you son. Maybe some day you will get to know how it feels to really hold your girl and dance with her. And you really, really, **really** need some dancing lessons boy."

"How you ever gonna know... if you never take the chance?"
"How you ever gonna know... if you never chase the dream?"

Atom was walking through a hell fire of prejudice by those who didn't want his kind to participate in any off campus activities. And worst of all, a guilt trip by Laura, his fiancée, they were *in love*.

Atom told her, "This is not goodbye I'll be back with you. But for now please allow me the privilege of doin' some runnin' around, and trying some new stuff. The only thing that will separate us is this new 'time' thing. Love is the basis of time, and we got love. Everyone here knows that we are one. There ain't nothing in that world to be afraid of. 'I was born to love you. Throughout all of creation you will always be my reason to Be. I will love you forever. ... Unconditionally. I promise."

Laura reluctantly told him to pursue his crazy pursuits, follow his ambitions, and live his dreams. She said she would pray for his safe return.

His Pop gave him a hug, told Atom that he was proud of him and that he loved him. Then his Dad said, Son, find out what works for you. You may not understand why, so... "Do what you got to do"...

Laura, contained her fury when he actually embarked on his adventure...
How could he leave her? She loved him and, He loved her, together they were perfect.
They were going to get married and live happy ever after. How could he scorn her this way?

Atom arrived on this "Earth" as the first human being. All that he needed was there for him. There was no want or greed. When he asked politely, the animals and plants gave their lives all he needed to survive on this "Island."

Atom could go anywhere, do anything, see and experience everything. Atom was an adventurous free spirit, enjoying the exercise of a human-<u>Being Alive.</u>

All was good in this virtual reality program. However, Atom had completed his goals on his list of adventures sooner than expected. He felt a big empty void in his heart. There was something missing. No matter where he searched, he couldn't find what he was looking for, because he wasn't sure what he was hunting for, but he kept trying to track it down like an old blue beagle hound.

Atom enjoyed his freedom, however he felt that it could all be better if he could share this life experience with the one he loved. A sunset is great, but a moment like that could be better shared with someone special. His friends couldn't get permission to sail on this ride with him, so he had to experience this adventure by himself or not at all. Spiritually he knew he was not alone. Physically he could survive by himself. The animals were his friends and companions. The communication lines to back home still had a free and clear connection. He could call his Pop any time day or night if things got hard to understand, or way out of hand.

The animals were good company; sometimes they were like clowns and made Atom laugh when they sensed he was feeling low. Yet he longed in his heart to share this great adventure of life with one of his own kind. He was lonely and really missed seeing his lovely Laura's smile. That smile made his heart beam brighter than any star.

However he had a nice little life. He had a little routine he liked. He parked a wrecked boat on a beach. Why he named it the 'Minnow' no body understood… He was free to go anywhere the days took him to. Although he had it all, all by himself, Atom felt the experiences could be more fulfilling if shared with someone else. There was something missing and in his heart he understood there was a difference in surviving and being alive.

The P.T.A., decided that it was time to send another human to this earth school. The next participant needed to be able to show Atom how to smell the roses.

Well, Laura missed him too. To her it felt they had been separated for a thousand lifetimes. She volunteered to enter the program and did so against the advise of her parents. They were afraid she could get stuck in the unbalanced energies of the Earth without a tether or tail to pull her back...

STYLE
Door # 5

Laura entered the program late in the afternoon. Her character was named Eve.

Do you wonder why she was named Eve?
Its very simple, she arrived in the evening during Atom's after dinner nap. If she had not chosen to be fashionably late, she would have been named Dawn.

Atom's heart was filled with joy as they watched the gift of a special sunset together.

As they viewed the sunset they knew it was a message from the other side that 'The Gift' of happiness was in their hands. Atom had seen many sunsets and this one was the best one yet.

A reproduction of this particular sunset is pictured on the back cover of this book.

Atom sang her the song from his heart about the Difference in "Living and Living Well." It was a big hit back home.

EARLY INTERMISSION

TAKE A BREAK,

STRETCH,

GET SOME WATER,

GO POTTY

WHATEVER!!!

I wanted to put the entire lyrics, to "Living and Living Well" by George
· Straight on this page.

But I was advised not to.

Sorry,
☹

Together they enjoyed running around, trying everything new, even flirted with disaster a few times. They ran like the wind, smiled like the sun, went places, saw things. Eve reminded Atom how to dare himself to dream. There was no desire to compete with each other. They were compLete. They had reunited with the secret ingredient of 'L'ove.

The young man reassured and promised his future in-laws he would bring their beautiful daughter back. Not to worry.

Atom didn't need to "go home." Home came to him. Love finally came to him. This was a perfect heaven on earth. Time spent with Eve was love. Their experience together verified what they were taught back home, Love is the basis of all time.

However, Atoms' lifestyle was in for a great change. Every destination they set out for, Atom wanted to get there in a hurry. Eve kept saying, "Whoa Man, slow down, smell these roses. Look at all the beauty around us." This frustrated Atom, because he wanted to get to his favorite fishing hole and all these scenic off ramps kept slowing him down. Everything worked out well. The fish were still there when they got there. Atom and Eve got to watch many sunrises and sunsets in their journeys.

Eve was always saying, (almost to the point of nagging) "Whoa Man." So all those who followed wanting to experience her energetic program were named Wo-Man.

The folks back home enjoyed watching their interaction. Atoms male energy was programmed to go get what he needs and move on. He would go to 'the store' and get what he went there for and go on.

Eve's feminine energetic program was much different. When she went to the 'store', she would look at everything, and eventually make a decision. Eve's way took too much time for Atom, she didn't know what she was looking for, but she assured him she would know what it was when she found it. He was getting a dancing lesson, which now included the new steps of patience and compromise.

Women go 'shopping.' Men go 'buying.' However there is one area that a man has received a special dispensation to go 'shopping'… the power tool, and or, the sporting goods section of any toy store.

PERNICIOUS INFLUENCE
Door # 6

All was perfect in this heaven on earth. Too perfect. There was a need to add a little excitement to this experiment, which had now evolved into a show being broadcast on one of the major Telephonygraph[19] Vision networks. The executives decided to add some little spices they called *pernicious*[20] *influences*[21] to the mixture…just for the fun of it!

Auditions were held and Atom's cousin Bubba made the staring character shine beyond their wildest imagination. He got the rockin' role, and had to spin it on his way to the Promised Land.

Everyone called him Bubba. His real name was Bartholomew Lawrence Zechariah BubouVonFrankinSteinO'VitchSki. a.k.a… B.L.Z.Bub.

Bubba happily assumed the character of the Villain. The program writers knew that you couldn't have a Hero without a Villain. It's basic soap opera drama 101.

Before Eve entered the program, she acknowledged that she knew what love was. Love was all that she had ever known. However she wished to experience that special facet of love called Forgiveness[ii].

---

[19] Telephonygraph: combination of two words; telephony and telephonograph ☺! **Telephony**: The use or operation of an apparatus for electrical transmission of sounds between widely removed points; as, wireless *telephony*. **Telephonograph**; a combination of a telephone receiver and a phonograph for recording and reproducing telephone messages. (Webster's 1961)
[20] Pernicious: Highly injurious or destructive in character; deadly. Intending or doing evil; wicked.
[21] Influences: has an effect upon. To produce an effect on by imperceptible or intangible means; sway.

Eve knew Bubba, and they agreed that if they both got a role on the show, Bubba would provide for her, a learning opportunity in forgiveness. What a classy…act…or…

"They" forgot to mention to Eve that forgiveness also includes self-forgiveness.

Bubba's mission was to split up the happy couple. This ingredient was intended to add a pinch of spicy intrigue to the dramatic premise. The ratings were projected to rise. If the plan worked during sweeps week, they could sweep the *meek*[22].

Before Bubba completely committed himself to the role of the villain, he made sure his contract was very clear. Although the veil of *"evil*[23]*"* mainly cloaked his character, he was still one of the good guys, offering an alternative 'life style.' There was a little spot of good on the inside. His Uncle (Gerry Garcia) explained it this way; "there's always a spot of light in the darkness, if you just look at it right."

On the wall of the control room an artist painted a picture that reminded everyone of this balanced world of "two lost souls swimming in a fish bowl, running around the same old ground, having found the same old fears." It was a symbol of the balance and duality, a symbol of *karma*[24]. The artist's intension was to paint a *metaphoric* [25]portrait intended to remind the players to look within and examine their own life.

---

[22] Meek: Easily imposed on; submissive.

[23] Evil: Injurious; mischievous. Morally corrupt; wicked. Producing or threatening sorrow, distress, or calamity. Arising from bad character, actual or imputed.

[24] Karma: In Hinduism and Buddhism, the whole ethical consequence of one's acts considered as fixing one's lot in the future existence. Hence, loosely, destiny; fate.

[25] Metaphor: A figure of speech in which a word or phrase literally denoting one kind of object or idea is used in place of another by way of suggesting a likeness or analogy between them.

The artist named it:
Yin and Yang
Subtitled: "Wish You Were Here"

This artist understood that an unexamined life is not worth living. When it came time for him to enter the program his character was also known as, Socrates.

When Bubba entered the program, he brought with him a trick or treat bag, and a sidekick. Every Super Villain, as well as a Super Hero, must have a sidekick. His character just wouldn't be complete without one. His sidekick's name was Pinkie. Bubba's favorite cartoon was "Pinkie and the Brain." Pinkie became his faithful assistant. He was the brain of the operation.

This bag of tricks was filled with tools of artificial intelligence. These tools were to be used to **e**dge good or **G**od **o**ut of the program. These tools were to be used to trap the human mind into believing that it is more intelligent than the consciousness that created it. The acronym for this artificial intelligence is, EGO.

Filled with cancerous viruses, these tricky temptations infected the players with amnesia. As these viruses reproduced, the players would forget who they really were. The victims became hypnotized and subject to Bubba's guidance in their futile attempt to find themselves.
The most powerful tool in this pharmaceutical attaché is the hallucinogenic venom of overwhelming unnecessary fear, which attempts to constrict the life out of you.

The only antidote to these toxins is Love. **<u>Unconditional Love.</u>** Unconditional Love is the governing law of the universe and is installed deep inside every program.

Bubba's mission was to inject his viruses and hide the antivenin.

He was wise enough to hide the antidote in a place where no one would ever look. He would conceal it right under their noses. It was obviously the safest hiding place.

As long as he could keep them looking outward, away from the truth in the heart of their soul, it would never be uncovered.

Generally, Bubba and Pinkie liked to play hide and seek with their childhood authority figures. "They were good ole boys. Never meaning no harm. It just seemed like; they been in trouble with the law from the day they were born."

If we choose to boldly go where we have never explored before. We can learn from the behavior of dogs. "If what you want is buried, dig until you find it."

In order to transmute fear and hate into love, sometimes ya gotta' dig really deep inside.

But if you dig too deep in trying to find it, and struggle by trying to understand every little detail. The prize you seek may elude you.

Bubba knew that digging was hard work. His strategy was; if he could *domesticate* [26] and *civilize* [27] these humans they would become very lazy, and that would make it easy to persuade the masses that someone else should do the difficult work for them. Bubba had the task of convincing everyone He was a grand excavator. He would do all the work for them. He said he would *safeguard* [28] their souls, (…from what?).

---

[26] Domesticate: tame

[27] Civilize: To cause to come out of a savage or barbarous state; to instruct in the customs of civilization; educate; refine.

[28] Safeguard: prevent from being harmed; protect. One that serves as protection or guard.

Their only contractual *obligation*[29] of this deal was *belief and faith* [30]in him.

The wheels of co-dependency stopped spinning, got gripsion, and started digging in.

Bubba's pharmaceutical bag was kind of like a backpack filled with emotional golf clubs, and fishing lures that he used to knock people off their center, or hook them. He had an iron for anger, rage, vengeance, hatred, and jealousy. Not to mention the cute little putter of safety, and huge drivers for judgment, self-judgment, and Fear. His tackle box had every gigging gadget imaginable.

All which are the tools of temptation, as well as self-discovery.

And, Well… (A deep thought for a shallow mind. Turn it sideways and you've got a tunnel)… of course this special bag contained a monster boom box full of musical tunes, and a keg of his favorite beer… on tap! He figured his life should be one big **PaaarTaaaay!**

Bubba's ultimate goal in this human-race: world domination, the elimination of inner peace, resulting in a complete *chaotic*[31] environment. His first

---

[29] Obligation: the state, fact or condition of being indebted to another for a special service or favor received; a duty, contract, promise or any other social, moral or legal requirement that binds one to follow or avoid a certain course of action; the sense of owning another.

[30] Belief: The state or habit of mind of one who believes; faith; confidence; trust; as to be without *belief* in God. A conviction or persuasion of truth; intellectual assent; as claims unworthy of belief. The thing believed; specif., a tenet, or body of tenets; doctrine; creed. **Syn.** Belief, faith, credence, credit mean the act or mental state of one who assents to something proposed for acceptance. **Belief and Faith,** though often used interchangeably are not quite parallel, for *belief* may or may not imply certitude in the one who assents *faith*, in its older religious and Scriptural sense, always does even when there is no evidence or proof. In current sense, *faith* often suggests credulity and overreadiness to accept. **Credence** stresses assent without implying, apart from the context; weak or strong grounds for belief or credulity or its absence; Credit implies assent on other grounds than direct proof, usually that of a reputation for truth in the one who proposed something for acceptance.

[31] Chaotic: Having the character, condition, place, or nature of total disorder or confusion.

mission was to separate these first two players, Atom and Eve, from each other and from their connection with their true essence.

Bubba's *learning*[32] process for the use of the combination of these tools was an evolutionary progression His job was to use any or all his tools, in various combinations to lure the players into *feeding*[33] on his temptations.

How one would react to Bubba's play determined their passageway into the future. It gave them an opportunity to make a choice.

The route (most unfavorable to Bubba) followed by responsible choice, would lead to *authentic*[34] power. Choice "A" is an existence knowing the oneness with all creation. It is a lifestyle that demonstrates the 3 R's. Respect for self, Respect for others, and Responsibility for all of your actions. It is a behavior pattern with the understanding and practice of the "*Golden Rule*[35]" and a positive karmic cycle.

Bubba celebrated each time someone blindly chose to follow his guilt trip induced guidance. a.k.a., choice "B."
Choice "B" is a road, which usually follows an unconscious or selfish decision based on a superficial *truth*[36]. It binds the individual to the path of

---

[32] Learning: is the process of obtaining new understandings and better ways to do things. Behavioral modification esp. through experience or conditioning.

[33] Feeding: Feed; To furnish something essential as to the growth, sustenance, or maintenance of.

[34] Authentic: having a genuine origin or authority; genuine; real. Trustworthy; credible; true.

[35] "The Golden Rule": although this is looked upon by Christians as Christian and is found the New and Old Testaments, many other races and peoples spoke of it. It also appears in the Analects of Confucius (fifth and sixth centuries B.C.) who himself, quoted from more ancient works. It is also found in "primitive" tribes. In one form or another it appears in the ancient works of Plato, Aristotle, Isocrates, and Seneca. For thousands of years it has been held by man as a standard of ethical conduct.

[36] Truth: That which agrees with the facts and observations; logical answers resulting from looking over all the facts and data; a conclusion based on evidence uninfluenced by desire, authority or prejudice; an inevitable (unavoidable) fact no matter how arrived at.

materialism[37], and its own revolving karmic cycle. This life-style is bound by the peristaltic chaos of contradictory thought and action.

The victims of dependency who follow the ways of choice "B", are usually testifying that it's always 'someone else's fault that their lives suck.' The map of choice "A" is never consulted for direction, because to do so would be an alternative responsible decision.

It's quite a perplexing karmic *phenomenon*. Some type of 'venge', revenge / avenge, is the perpetual force that keeps these wheels turning. Forgiveness is *pilloried*[38] and considered a weakness. And we all know that sometimes forgiveness of self and others requires the force of Super-human strength.

---

[37] Materialism: The theory or attitude that only physical well-being and the acquisition of worldly possessions constitute the greatest good and highest value in life. The theories seek to explain away things as minds by saying they can be reduced to physical things or their motions. Materialism is a very ancient idea. There are others, i.e., String theory.

[38] Pilloried: exposed to ridicule, public contempt, scorn or abuse. Pillory: a wooden framework on a post, with holes for the head and hands, in which offenders were formerly locked to be exposed to public scorn as punishment.

The Entangled Threads of Time
Door # 7

As we practice the *examples*[39] of what we perceive to be *virtues*[40], either out of obligation, or *incompetence*[41], in an attempt to *honor*[42] the ways of our mentors, we are constantly faced with choices. These choices can have a positive or negative effect on our *survival*[43], environment, and *happiness*[44]. What worked well yesterday may be missing a piece to get it to operate today, and upgrades or purification may be needed for it to survive tomorrow.

We have been programmed for generations by many leading aristocracies to *parrot*[45] the theory that only one *lineal*[46] time line or reality exists. Humbly accepting their "say so."
Past_____Present_____Future.

Each choice we make leads to future realities along a *facet* [47]of that particular lineal time line frequencies. However, everything happens in the <u>Now</u>, past, present, and futures are simultaneous reactions. There are an infinite

---

[39] Examples: someone, something, or some pattern of behavior worthy of imitation or duplication; a pattern, a model, or precedent.

[40] Virtues: the ideal qualities in good human conduct.

[41] Incompetence: lacking adequate knowledge or skill or ability; unskilled; incapable; subject to making big errors or mistakes; bungling.

[42] Honor: to show respect for, to treat with deference and courtesy.

[43] Survival: the act of remaining alive, continuing to exist, of being alive.

[44] Happiness: a condition or state of well-being, contentment, pleasure; joyful, cheerful, untroubled existence; the reaction to having nice things happen to one.

[45] Parrot: A person who repeats words or patterns of behavior, mechanically without understanding.

[46] Lineal: Consisting of or being in, a direct line of ancestry or descendants; -opp., to *collateral*. Derived from ancestors in the direct line; hereditary.

[47] Facet: one of the small plane surfaces of a diamond or other cut gem or of a crystal. A phase or aspect, as of a topic.

number of intertwined braided *collateral*[48] time line fibers. In his own way, our Einstein figured this out.

The programmers kept developing new computer type technologies to keep track of all the variations and the ripple side effects of events each individual choice would lead to or away from.

The emerging growth in the equipment needed to follow and keep track of all of the long spiraling transversal lines of these collateral intertwined time strands; created such a large explosion (a big bang) in the co-creative industry that the High School couldn't handle it any more. So they moved everything to a place they called the Universe City.

The different courses of learning possibilities of each choice were given their own frequency band, just like the programmed realities of radio and television channels. On one channel back home one might be able to watch these soapy dramas we are role-playing at this time. Other channels might broadcast 'reality' shows based on some of these plots;
If Adolph Hitler (Bubba) would have won World War II, if the Apes ruled this planet, if humans learned from a man who was crucified for showing the way of forgiveness, compassion, kindness, and love. And another channel will show how your life might have been different if you followed the truth in your heart, instead of running away from it in search for something better. And yet another channel might be showing this story with the gender roles reversed. There are infinite possibilities.

The catch is; any time a player (student experiencing this earth school) changes its mind and makes an attempt to pursue choice "A," Bubba has to play defense in order to survive. Bubba's best defense is an *implacable*[49] *adamant*[50] offence.

---

[48] Collateral: Parallel; side by side, as collateral fibers.
[49] Implacable: not open to being quieted, soothed or pleased; remorseless; relentless.
[50] Adamant: hard, not giving in; stubbornly unyielding; something which won't break; insistent; refusing any other opinion; surrendering to nothing.

And now the player must find ways to defend its self from Bubba's overwhelming chaotic attacking forces. The individual must be willing to release control to the Great Spirit (God), even if it feels that he or she is unsupported by family and friends in a sole battle for soul control. It requires some sacrifice.

In order to bail off the ride down path "B" and return to flight path "A" one must make the choice and clear the static of Bubba's *propaganda*[51] from the data processor known as your brain and ask your higher self for guidance.

Your Higher Self is like you're out of body, video game player from the other side. It may be you, who is observing your little drama from a higher vantage point, the cheap seats. Working the joystick assisting with guidance when requested, and protection when your clouded judgment makes you act in a manner that jeopardizes the life of your *destiny*[52].

Guidance from this level of consciousness can only be given if the player asks for it, and can only be received if the mind is open and has freed a space, in its 'hard drive' to receive it.

To some the higher self may also be known as the superconscious.[53]

This interaction works just like computers, the answers that manifest are to the exact questions or instructions (intensions / prayers) you send to it. Sometimes you need to update the directions when you discover that you left out one little detail or keystroke. Ya get exactly what you ask for, determined by the way you request or command and the key actions that follow.

Thanks for logging on to this little story. Hang on; we're diving back into the drama… or trauma?

---

[51] Propaganda: spreading ideas, information or rumor to further one's own cause and/or injure that of another, often without regard to the truth; the act of putting lies in the press or on radio and TV so that when a person comes to trial he will be found guilty; the action of falsely damaging a person's reputation so he will not be listened to.

[52] Destiny: the predetermined course of events often conceived as a resistless power of agency; fate.

[53] Superconscious: That part of the higher soul structure which is usually unconscious but accessible to the personality. The superconscious contains higher wisdom, whereas the subconscious relates to the personality of a six year old. (Vibrational Medicine Richard Gerber, M.D.)

Search for Discovery
Door # 8

Atom and Eve weren't informed of the new gaming revolution and Bubba's spiraling roll in it. It was something they had to discover for themselves. Surprise! Surprise!

Bubba knew that if he told Atom and Eve the truth, he couldn't get them to do what he needed them to. Atom and Eve loved each other; it was a Spiritual Love, a bond that absolutely nothing on Earth could break. Their souls were united in the heavens above.

Bubba would attempt to *vandalize*[54] this thing called love. It wasn't anything personal. It's just the forked contractual points of his tale.

When Bubba showed up he first met with Atom. Atom and Bubba laughed each time the other farted, it's just a male bonding theme. Fortunately for them, neither of them had any matches…

They built a small shelter and did a tenant finish on a cave one week. It was to be a weekend getaway for Atom and his family. As they stacked one stone over two, the construction industry was born. Friends and family of Atom and Eve no longer looked down upon them as, single home parents.

After they finished the project Atom washed his body in a stream. Then invited his new acquaintance to have dinner with him, his lovely wife Eve, and son Able.

Bubba asked Atom, why did they name the child Able? Atom told him that his son had some exceptional abilities right from birth, so they named him Able.

---

[54] Vandalism: the willful and malicious destruction of public or private property, especially anything beautiful or artistic.

Bubba didn't take a bath this first week on earth. No need to bathe back home; never got dirty. However, these electro-biological machines, these flesh bodies, developed and produced unpleasant emissions. Bubba hadn't yet read the part of his owner's manual for care and cleaning of his vehicle.

Eve immediately become nauseated the moment she met Bubba. He was a dirty, smelly, *boorish*[55], and horny creature.

Eve was a Babe! Bubba sported a woody the entire time he was in her presence. He thought he was complementing her when he told her she had a 'phat' ass. He wanted to "do" her! She wouldn't have any part of him. Atom demanded he leave before the meal was finished.

Atom sensed that something had changed in the environment. It was something they had never encountered before. He felt the presence of a negative energy that could *deter*[56] the survival of their happiness. Atom told Eve to steer clear of that man, something's just not right about him.

Bubba departed that evening for his first night with himself, lonely and horny. He was feeling sad and rejected. He was really bummed out because the only one he had to play with... was him self. However he discovered one little joy!

When he hand polished his little unique horn, it would stand tall at attention, this relief gave him great pleasure!

He was jealous because his manhood couldn't measure up to Atoms. Bubba was experiencing the side effects of his overuse of 'magic dust' from a previous life experience. But he was such the big little man.

He began to sing, "double the pleasure, double the fun! I wish I had Two Pricks instead of just one!" Unde POOF! Bubba became...a horny little devil.

---

[55] Boorish: implies rudeness of manner, insensitiveness to others' feelings, or unwillingness to make oneself agreeable. A rude, clumsy person with little refinement.

[56] Deter: to prevent or discourage. To prevent or discourage the occurrence of an action, as by means of fear and doubt.

Unfortunately he got what he asked for, not what he meant. He had manifested two bony protuberances sticking out of his forehead. He now has to wear many hats to hide them when he appears in public.

Bowtie Bookies
Door # 9

Bubba and Pinkie played a round of golf the next day. Pinkie caddied.

While on the golf course, Bubba sang along with the tunes from the boom box on his golf bag. Eventually, he attached a microphone to project his voice from this music box.
He called it **Karaoke!**[iii] It's why he was banished from heaven. Various books of metaphors and parables, tell a different story. In truth, it was Karaoke that led to Bubba being kicked out of the heavens. Simon says; some voices were just not meant to sing. Period. Enough said.

Pinkies caddying buddies were watching this show on their TV in the caddie shack. They started making bets with each other if Bubba would "Score" with Eve or not. Side bets of when Pinkie would pick his nose. The payoff would double if Pinkie ate the bugger.

The executives of this new game were getting real excited about the increasing rating of the show. There were a lot of wagers being entered in little books at a deserted area where the Last 'Vegas' were parked.

So they sent a message to Bubba that he couldn't refuse. If you can get Eve to <u>allow</u> you to rape her, your compensation will proliferate immensely.

The rule is: Eve must allow Bubba to rape her; he couldn't force his ill will in her. She must give him permission. She must do so by free will. So Bubba had to figure out how to seduce her. This added a challenge to this new scenario. Bubba would have to use many tools of deception in order to receive the additional achievement perks for success in his performance. He was hell bent to get one of them OS-cars, power stroked by an Emmy. They're the best!

Sex sells, and Eve wanted to experience that special part of love known as forgiveness…Remember?

Bubba went to work. He got his body cleaned up. Built a bigger shelter, customized a huge cave, it's like one of today's mansions or cathedrals. Built high on a hill with a spectacular view. He created some very comfortable furniture. The palace had all the fixin's. You name it; it had it. But could these fluffy flashy things lure Eve away form Atom's love?

Why should Eve sleep on the hard ground when she could come here and stay in a place with a soft comfortable bed, indoor heat, an indoor bathing room with hot water, a heated box to cook food instead of over an open fire. It was safe and secure. He figured Eve would definitely sell out for this comfortable lifestyle.

However, Eve's life now was comfortably safe and secure, she knew no different. She had no fears. Eve was happy being where she was, she had all she needed, and she had love.

"Got to make her feel crazy, so I can make her feel secure," Bubba thought. He created great walls around this mansion, to keep all the 'bad' things out. He had to re-spin the camouflage of his villain cloak, so He could be her Hero!

Clean shirt, new shoes… Gold watch, diamond rings. He was about to steal her Zen[57]… Bubba was looking sharp and looking for wuv. Because "Every Girl Crazy about a Sharp Dressed Man!" Shhhhh… be verwy verwy quiet.

---

[57] Zen: A Buddhist teaching asserting that enlightenment can be attained through meditation, self-contemplation, self-discipline, and through direct intuitive insight.

Bubba magically mastered the *cant* [58]of the human buck in rut. He was hungry and on a mission... to get bred, bread, and $bread!

Bubba visited the happy couple and their son a few times to see if they recognized him in his new costume. He even had them over for dinner. During this dinner party they talked about the new people that were filtering into this adventure land. They chatted about the 'bum' that came by earlier that season. Bubba said that the dissolute man did some work around his place and just vanished one day. They all wondered what happened to him.

That night as the happy family traveled home from dinner with their 'friend', Atom couldn't shake the feeling that Bubba had the scent of a buck in rut. Eve didn't smell it. Bubba gave her some perfume, (it covered up his truc scent). The flowery fragrances made the little bunny feel delightfully fuzzy.

Atom mentioned to Eve that he felt that something was out of balance with Bubba. He told his lovely partner to be cautious around him. He said, I'm not sure what it is, but there's something about him that's not quite 'light'. Eve didn't believe him.

"There's nothing wrong with Elmer! YOU Just **think** there's something wrong!" Eve adamantly protested. She said that this is a perfect world of peace, love and sheer happiness and there's nothing to be concerned about. Eve was a little infatuated with the exciting appearance of all Bubba's worldly comforts. Plus Bubba played music and sang for her.
She thought that Bubba had a stellar voice! He was a much better singer than Atom!

In another time frame, there is a rumor that Milli Vanilli used Bubba's entertaining format as the foundation for their musical career.

---

[58] Cant: The expression particular to, and generally understood only by, members of a particular sect, class, or occupation; as: The secret jargon of thieves, tramps, etc.

Atom's concern came from the depths of his souls intuition; it wasn't just a whimsical notion.

He felt that something was attempting to tap into their life force energy and drain it. He wondered if Bubba was a vampire. Not the kind of blood sucking creatures he watched on scary movie night back home, but a new breed of vampire.

The odds were leaning in Bubba's favor. The bookies were juggling a lot of betting combinations. Atom and Eve staying together was becoming a real long shot.

Crisis Connoisseur
Door # 10

The animals posed no threat to Atom and Eve; there was nothing to be afraid of. So Bubba disguised himself as an animal with a 'short circuit' and prowled around, creating great concern from Atom and Eve.

Disguised as a wild cat, Bubba started vandalizing the area around their home. He even tried to kidnap Able one time. He didn't want to injure the child, just place real fear into his parents. Able just wanted to play with the furry kitty cat. Mom and Dad knew that this rabid creature posed a health risk not only to itself, but to other lives it may contact.

Bubba did an excellent job of 'creating a crisis' to raise their fear with a new level of distraction.

Atom and Able were away from home one day, repairing the damage this one 'bad cat' had done.

Bubba saw his window of opportunity! Eve was alone. So Der Slickmister slid right into their home. He started his smooth talk. Oh how this budding cunning linguist fluctuated the truth!

On his way to see Eve, Bubba stopped and talked to Atom and Able. But we'll bounce back to that act later.

Eve was real crazy about Bubba's appearance. Atom never got all fancied up like this dude. As the two visited, Bubba gave her some more special perfume. She liked it. He hoped it would have an aphrodisiac effect. Eve noticed that Bubba was wearing lots of beautiful rings that glistened with the light. As they laughed and talked, Bubba slid in some very complementary flattery. This rhetoric impressed Eve to a point where she got all giggly.

Ding! Ding! Ding! The window of opportunity just opened a, whittle wider!

Bubba asked her, why such a beautiful woman as she, was left all alone?

She explained that there was a sick cat out there, and that her husband and son were out looking for it. And when they found it they were going to take it to get some healing attention.

With great sincerity, Bubba told Eve that if he had a partner as gorgeous as her, He would never leave her alone. There is something dangerous lurking about out there.
(hee hee hee hee)
It's probably not safe for you to be all alone he said. The seed of doubt was planted.

Now all Bubba had to do was sit back, water it a bit, and watch as his fruits of fear begin to blossom.

Bubba inquired about where Atom and Able went searching.
She told him.
Immediately Bubba got a shockingly concerned look on his face.
She asked, "Why? Why do you have that look on your face? What is it?"
She started feeling worried.
He told her that in his travels he wondered up to what looked like a dead human body, and gave a vague description.
Eve went into an emotional state of shock. It got worse when he showed her a torn bloody piece of clothing Able was wearing. He told her that he heard a child screaming in pain. But when he got there, all he found was this bloody rag. The sick animal must still be out there.

Eve was afraid, horrified. She believed that her family was dead, and she was now completely alone in this world.
Her anxiety was a great comfort to Bubba. His horror-to-culturist skills were flowering.

Oh, yes it was true Bubba had seen Atom that day. They had talked about the 'renegade critter'. However what transpired was much different than the story Bubba told Eve.

Well, you see, as the two men were talking, Able ran up to his dad crying and whining about his pain. Able had tripped and skinned his shin, and it was bleeding. It wasn't anything serious, just messy, didn't need any stitches. You know how kids are…you used to be one.

Atom showed Able how to clean and bandage the wound. He used part of the boy's shirt for a bandage. Good ole dad was showing his son how to improvise and use what he has at the moment as a quick fix until you get to a place where things can be done properly.
It was a lesson in first aid.

It just so happened that Bubba told them that he had a gift for the boy. Just like magic, he manifested a new shirt out of his bag and gave it to Able. It was a perfect fit!

Some things just make you go hmmmm…

Bubba told Atom he had seen the critter miles away resting in a valley. He took a stick and drew a map on the ground so Atom could get a good idea where to go. When Bubba finished drawing the map, it looked like a vague outline of a body lying on the ground…

Atom didn't pay much attention to the artistic image of the map; Able was working on his crying scene…intentionally.

Bubba suggested that they part ways, each taking a different side of the mountain and circle in to "bag" the sick one. And together they would take it to get proper attention. Then grab a beer or two.
He told Atom to wait in a certain spot, hold a light, and he would get the animal to run to him.

For days Atom and son circled far and wide and finally settled into position and waited for Bubba to herd the animal toward him. Basically this tryst was the first snipe hunt. And Atom and Able were the first victims of… beer pressure.

Good ole Bubba, not wanting to litter the earth, picked up the bloody rag when Atom wasn't looking.

Golly, Bub sure left out a few minor details in the story he told to Eve.
Eve felt in her heart that what she had just heard was not true. However the emotional stress she was experiencing created a barrier splitting the connection of her heart and mind. She was being torn apart inside.

Bubba was very persuasive. His appearance was impeccable. He was well groomed, handsome, intelligent, articulate, extremely well mannered, and so caring and compassionate. He could sing, and his hands were soft, unlike Atoms. When Atom cautioned her about Bubba she thought that he was just jealous. At that time she felt that something was wrong with her husband because of his concerned attitude.
She could trust Bubba, however she was becoming unsure about her husband. He wasn't a pretty boy like Bubba.

As Eve cried on Bubba's shoulder, he held in his inner grin. He offered to take Eve back home with him. She would be safe there. He promised he would protect and provide for her. All she needed to do was to trust him.

Bubba had preyed on her fear and insecurity and it worked! He even convinced her not to go to the place where he had seen the body. He said, 'believe' me the sight would be too horrifying for you.
Eve didn't even consider investigating this tragedy for herself. She didn't question anything. She listened to Bubba, and made her choice based solely on the information he gave her. She assumed, thereby avoiding any confrontation with the true feelings of her heart felt intuition. Eve was so rattled that she didn't pay attention to the raucous voices of the crows and ravens that were sounding an alarm.

Hoodwinked
Door # 11

When they arrived at Bubba's home, Eve felt very grateful that she had been taken to such a safe, peaceful and secure place. She was totally impressed with the excessive abundance of everything. Yet she was still mourning in her heart for the loss of her beloved husband and son. Bubba gave her space.

Whirlwinds of seduction scenarios were spinning in Bubba's head. Knowing that honesty would get him absolutely nowhere, Bubba patiently and compassionately told Eve the things she wanted to hear.

The honesty thing would only escort Eve into leaving, and he would just be sitting there alone, rejected again, hand buffing his wood. And he didn't want to go through carpal tunnel surgery… again. He wanted to score!

Bubba told her that this new lifestyle would continue to be hers if she stayed with him, did as He said, without question. He promised her complete safety, a life of ease, filled with all the comforts this world could provide. These selling points were beginning to sound real good to Lady Eve.

More days passed and Eve was giving Bubba the cold shoulder anytime he got a little too emotionally or physically close.

He had to get her to drop her guard completely. He was slowly wearing her down, he knew that eventually the time would arrive, but he wanted it to come… now.
And the edema of Bubba's little finger needed to be soaked in cider to stop the painful itching and twitching. It was difficult to quietly handle this distraction.

What to do? What to do? Eve is way too quiet. He looked into his bag of tricks. I need something help persuade her to let her guard down, and unlock her lips.

I need something pretty, and sparkly, with happy bubbles that will tickle her nose, and her fancy. He reached into his dark magic bag, and guess what... he pulled out a bottle of golden sparkling cider.

That evening by the flickering firelight they sipped this delightful champagne. It was so romantic. Eve was becoming intoxicated. Bubba decided that it was time to put the icing on the cake. He told her he loved her. She melted, and All resistance...Gone.
CHING! CHING! He scored!!! It was the world's first one night stand.

Eve took the hook, swallowed the bait, and acrobatically bobbed the knob. Not only did she get hammered in more ways than one, she got pregnant; Bubba received extra bonus bucks for the reproduction. Not to mention he got to keep the piece of her soul that he had *hoodwinked*[59] from her. What a Trophy!

---

[59] Hoodwink: To deceive.

Naaaas Car! Dude...
Door # 12

The show was a home run hit with the viewing public. It was decided to expand the game. They sectioned the playing field into four quarters. Assembled four expansion teams and designated playing fields to each team. The four corners of the earth had been established.

A review of the decision as to who was on what team, they gave different skin colors to the players on each of the four teams. There was black, red, yellow and white. These were the primary skin 'colors' that were used to identify the original *gangs*[60] or tribes of individuals.

The chassis and drive trains of these body machines for these four "races" were built from a master plan, so to speak. The anatomies are the same. However these mechanical machines are designed to survive and adapt to the particular environmental track they were running on and the roles they signed up to play.

In addition to the interior commonalities there is a little surprise located at the deepest layer of the skin. At this deepest layer of epidermis there are special cells known as melanocytes. These unique cells are the manufacturers of a protein called melanin. Melanin is what gives the skin its hue / color, and protection from the sun's ultraviolet radiation.

Team Bubba has tried to *deter* this little secret... All human body machines have something in common; they have the same number of melanocytes per square mm of skin. It is the rate of synthesis of melanin that is different in each human racing machine...

---

[60] Gang: A company of persons acting together for some purpose.

This little known fact might have a powerful *influence* with our *hereditary*[61] *precepts*[62] of "W.A.R".[iv]

These body machines are shaped and programmed for specific purposes and learning experiences. Big, small, short, tall, lean, round… each brings a specific talent or gift that could be used to complete, or *compete* [63]with the team group they are in. It is a constantly evolving process of environmental adaptation and communication within the varieties of external body styles of the similar and varied *species*[64].

---

[61] Hereditary: Descended, or capable of descending, from an ancestor to an heir at law. Transmuted, or transmissible, as a constitutional quality or condition from parent to offspring.

[62] Precepts: rules or statements advising or laying down a principle or principles or a course of action regarding conduct; directions meant as a rule for conduct.

[63] Compete: its action is to gain power over, it has no love. Complete has love, the "L".

[64] Species: A category of classification lower than a genus or sub genus and above a subspecies or variety; a group of animals or plants which possess in common one or more distinctive characters, and do or may interbreed and reproduce their distinctive characters in their offspring.

Life in the WOK
Door # 13

Many understand life in the 'The Wheel of Karma'. Round and round it goes, will it stop, No-body knows.

Participants get to experience the life long effects of following flight path "A", off road through rocky-way "B", or any multiple scenic combinations of the two forces fields.

Love.

Fear.

Love of fear.

Fear of love.

Love of the fear of love, etc., etc…

Each choice gives the individual the opportunity to *learn* from the experience and move on to another level of consciousness. Or be held back until they choose to receive the desire and ability to learn the lesson they came to receive. Or, continue their practice of the message of compassion.

Every decision may lead to a corresponding reality *incarnation*[65]or a different parallel *reincarnation*[66]. The consequences of a decision in one relationship will resurface to be experienced in another. The individual or groups get to experience the behavioral influence of that individual or collective decision. The effect of everything will eventually come back and experienced. For better or worse, naughty or nice, rich or poor, sick or healthy, loving or hateful, forgiveness lesson provider or forgiveness lesson receiver, however

---

[65] Incarnation: An incarnating; a clothing, or state of being clothed, with flesh. Any concrete or actual form incorporating or exemplifying a principle, ideal, or the like; esp., a person showing a trait or typical character to a marked degree.

[66] Reincarnation: The belief that the souls of the dead successively return to earth in new forms or bodies. The rebirth of the soul in another body. A reappearance or revitalization in another form; a new embodiment. Authors simplified interpretation: One who has not successfully learned a life lesson, a lesson that will be repeated until it is learned, repeated until it is learned… a.k.a. B.O.H.I.C.A.

you do unto others you shall receive. In one relationship or an other. It's only *karma*[67]!

---

[67] Karma: In Hinduism and Buddhism, the whole ethical consequence of one's acts considered as fixing one's lot in the future existence. Hence, loosely, destiny; fate.

Monkey Business
Door # 14

Lets ride the pinball back over to Eve's little personal drama.

As she was slowly awakening, with quite the nauseous hangover, a winged messenger, an angel appeared in her room. This brightly colored little bird whispered in her ear. It told her that Atom and Able were alive and she had been deceived.

Eve not only felt ashamed, but also was suffering from the fever of self-judgment compounded by a gilt trip that Bubba had hanging over her head. Adding insult to injury… she was having a bad hair day.

Eve was stepping lightly like a woodpecker with a headache, as she attempted to sneak her way out of Bubba's *domain*[68]. Staying out of Bubba's sight wasn't hard to do; his attention spotlight was occupied.
He was a little too busy to focus on Eve due to his exasperating attempts to chase a strange monkey out of the chicken coop.

She recognized this obnoxious monkey; it was her mini-kid cousin Art.

Art was throwing magic monkey eggs at Bubba. These 'eggs' were grenades of truth. When an egg hit ole Bubba, it temporarily short-circuited the illusion of his force field like peeling an onion. Bubba hates it when this shit hits him.

Eve saw a recognizable layer of the character Bubba was playing. She saw that disgusting horny boorish man that Atom brought home for dinner… and cautioned her about.

---

[68] Domain: As estate held in possession; landed estate. The territory over which dominion is exerted; hence, sphere of action, thought, influence, etc.

Art was having too much fun keeping Bubba, a.k.a. Sonny, busy so his cousin could get away. Every time an egg hit its target Art would laugh and yell, "Oooo Oooo Aaaa Aaaa, The yolk's on you… Man!" It was a zinging rain of truth that fanned through the air.

Even though these spheres of truth allowed Eve to see through a filter of his illusion they didn't have the power to unveil the entire phenomenon of Bubba's character. She couldn't see that old friend who agreed to allow her the experience of total forgiveness.

Eve was humiliated, very angry and disappointed with herself. She thought she was soooo smart. How could she be so stupid, so blind, and so vulnerable? Bubba stroked her emotions like he was delicately playing a beautiful harp sonata. He scored with a bluff and cashed in holding only a pair of duce's'. Deduce and seduce.

What a float trip!
Door # 15

But it never happened…

When Eve arrived at her house Atom was waiting there for her. He had absolutely no knowledge of Eve's recent incident. He said they couldn't find the cat. Eve kept her usual cool composure when she told Atom that she felt it was time to move. She felt it was not safe for them to live in this neighborhood any longer. Eve wouldn't explain why she felt this way and just brushed it off as her woman's intuition. That was a good enough explanation for Atom, so the family moved. They moved far away and settled in an area they thought was superb. Yes, they actually fled to superbia. Golly, Imagine that…

Eve kept her humiliating incident with Bubba buried deep inside. She chose to evade facing the traumatic episode by denying to herself that it ever happened. The saddle of invalidating any notion that she carried any personal responsibility for her experience created a stressful rift in the equilibrium between her heart and mind. She was afraid that if Atom would become aware, he would stop loving her. And the last thing she wanted to hear was, 'I told you so.'

Unconditional Love was not a sure thing to Eve anymore. She hated how Bubba had used her, and couldn't forgive him for whatever it was that he had sheered away from her. The love she once had for herself was fading, and in this growing emptiness, her feeling of self worth was being fattened with the fixation to obtain the luxuries Bubba tempted her with.

Atom observed the slight changes in Eve's behavior; he felt that something was out of balance. When he gently asked her if something was wrong, she would say, "nothing" and she just walked away or demanded that he conjure up some thing extravagant.

Her love for Atom was becoming conditional upon the tangible objects he could provide for her. The harder he worked, the more he provided, never seemed to be enough. The love and tenderness that he showered her with was nullified and *discarded.*[69] Eve was looking for the golden things Atom could give her but couldn't see that the gold she was digging for was the love in his golden heart. The unhappier she became inside, the more she looked to external pleasures and excitement to fill the growing void. This had an adverse effect because her dis-ease grew and grew, and the fire inside her heart became very cold. Bubba's venom was *transmuting*[70] her into a "Material Girl" living in a material world.

Eve's entire being was comforted with a quilt of rosy eyed innocence that cuddled the insecurities she had gestating inside herself. She felt that it was Atoms fault for what happened to her. Not only did he go out chasing some strange pussy…cat, what really pissed her off was, what he told her about Bubba…was right. This made her so mad that she felt like she could just explode.

Eve felt unsafe in this world of duality. She felt like all masculine human energy was going to attack and devour her. In order to avoid being rode hard and put up wet, she entombed herself into the sanctuary of her own little world. She was afraid to touch people, and afraid of being touched. So she shut her self off. She closed the door and was afraid to receive the true love that was waiting to be delivered through Atom. She battled back and forth within her mind, with something that she felt was much bigger and stronger than she could rise above. Her soul was in a competition with the ego-ogre.

She shot the angry arrows of her frustrations toward Atom and Able. They were the men that were supposed to protect her. However they couldn't protect her from herself.

---

[69] Discarded: Discard; to cast off as useless or as no longer of service; to reject. Implies the getting rid of that which had become an annoyance, an interference, or the like.

[70] Transmute: To change from one nature, form, substance, or species, into another; convert.

Unfortunately these arrows were being shot in the wrong direction, so they missed their target, it was a terribly original *sin*[71].

She once knew the ways of a loving world. When Eve and Atom made love with each other they experienced the joys of giving and receiving, they were participants practicing a loving *s*ynergistic *e*nergy e*x*change (S.E.X.).[v]

Bubba introduced Eve to a new way of life when he fucked her. She was no longer capable of giving or receiving unconditional love. This was a living death sentence. She had just been introduced to the world of give and take by this ungodly monster. The connection to the other side was severed. She was no longer a part of, but apart from what they called G.O.D. God is love. Without this connection, As long as she continued to fear God, fear love…she could not return home. Love is God.

Well… needless to say, that titillating dance serving Bubba didn't do much for her self-esteem. But it sure was fun!

Eve's infection surfaced through spoiled childish *tyrannical*[72] *aristocratic*[73] behavior patterns proved to be a real challenge for her family.

Her behavior became very vague and scattered. Sometimes Yes meant No, and No meant Yes. This conduct was very confusing to her family. Atom and Able couldn't do anything to her satisfaction. When either of them asked, "which is it Yes or No?" Eve just replied, "you should know!" Eve didn't know where any boundaries were, and was scared to make any decision because she feared the personal repercussions that came with a simple yes, or, no. She was so angry with Bubba; she couldn't see how her life had been turned around. She was screwing herself deeper into the chaotic madness.

---

[71] Sin: To sin, archaic archery term, interpreted to mean, to miss the mark, to miss the target. The theologian Rheinhold Niebuhur declared that sin is a separation from the truth.

[72] Tyrannical: the use of cruel, unjust and absolute power; crushing; oppressing; harsh; severe.

[73] Aristocratic: A group who can make or apply laws to others but consider that they themselves are immune to the laws, or code of conduct.

A river was named in honor of Eve's condition. Many human life times are spent on this scenic trip, as they float down the river of denial. Afraid to wonder or ask…Why?

Eve's behavior was stressing her family to the breaking point. One time Able was given something to eat. The item looked unfamiliar. When he asked his mom what it was, she said it was a potato. Able had eaten a lot of potatoes in his life and he knew this wasn't a potato. It didn't look like a potato; it didn't smell like a potato, it wasn't a potato. He knew his mom was lying to him and wouldn't eat the damn thing because she was lying. They had a huge argument. Eve was very unhappy with Able calling her bluff by questioning her… 'Said-so'. It was so disrespectful.

Eve in a conniption fit of frustration screamed at Able, "If I told you what it was, you wouldn't eat it!" She was afraid that if she told her son the truth, he wouldn't do what she wanted him to do, (swallow the deception).

Able didn't have anything against turnips he actually liked them. But this one was different from those he had encountered before. He didn't know it but this turnip was one of the gifts Bubba brought his family that fateful day. This one had been genetically and energetically altered. The nutrition of this food if digested and introduced into his body would have caused the reproduction of his mothers dis-ease in the young lad.

Atom was hungry when he got home late from a hard days work. Food… Eat.

Ables' disobedience was a painful test of his strength of character. It was his first step forward on his life path rejecting a life-style that required blindly honoring the double standard codes of *nobility's*[74] hypocrisy.

Able left home immediately after this clash with his Mom. He went on a walk about searching for something that would heal her. He loved her and

---

[74] Nobility: Quality or state of being noble in character, ability, rank, etc., Noble: Of high birth or exalted rank station; aristocratic; as, *noble* blood, birth.

it was too painful to see his mom in her current condition. He went and sat on a hill to talk to his Grandfather, and cried for help.

Antique E-Mail
Door #16

Able had seen his Pop do this many times when he needed help with something. Atom had explained to Able the steps to take to get a free and clear connection when he wished to communicate with his ancestors on the other side. He remembered a lullaby his Poppa (grandfather) used to sing to him.

"If life gets hard to understand, and your life's getting out of hand…
Come to Poppa, Come see your Poppa…"

The young boy sat on that hill crying for days. Until, he suddenly spotted something unusual floating in the sky. It grabbed his attention. It looked like his Grandpa's handwriting, but it was backwards. It took a while for Able to understand that he was reading this skywriting from the other side of the window.

It looked like, "*ᑐ ᖇᓕᑫ Ꭵᗰ*"

But it read, "*Hi Kola !*" [75]

This was an AhhHaa moment for the young lad.

When he yelled "HI GRANDFATHER!" a light breeze gently erased the writing clearing the sky, acknowledging the line of communication was

---

[75] Kola: friend in Lakota (Oglala) dialect. Koda: friend in Dakota dialect.

open. Then his old friend began to write him a message on the slate of the virgin bluc canvas.

His Grandpa continued,

Little Friend

I give you the Serenity to accept the things you cannot change.

&,

The Courage to change the things you can.

&,

The Wisdom to know the difference.

Have a Fun, and Safe adventure.

Happy Trails...

With love,

Tunkashilah

Another Phase?
Door # 17

Atom was working like a slave as Eves demands increased. He was so busy working that he didn't have any time to contribute to this woman that he loved with his whole being. Eve missed the closeness and intimacy they once shared, their relationship was becoming way too serious. However, her addiction to the alternative exciting lifestyle was enhancing the shields that were deflecting the unconditional love of the universe that was being channeled to her, through Atom.

Eve became what one would consider a non-materialistic hypocrite. She self-importantly made this statement to Atom, "My world is peace, love, and pure happiness." Followed by a real ass chewing about how worthless Atom was, and how the tangible things and adventures he shared with her, could never measure up to what Bubba could provide.

Atom tried to show Eve his love by attempting to provide the stuffing she demanded. He thought it was just a phase she was going through and she would eventually grow out of it. He made a spectacular pond in the back yard. He gave her a magnificent horse, and even the most lavish mode of transportation imagined, a camel. This was no ordinary camel, in its climate controlled riding enclosure, it had heated soft leather seats, a killer sound system, a DVD player for the kids, tinted windows to keep the sun's ultraviolet rays out, beverage holders and an ice box, it even had its own automatic pilot. All she had to do was tell the camel where she wanted to go, sit back and enjoy the ride.

Atom had become Eve's beast of burden. It didn't matter how much love he placed into everything he did for her; she couldn't be satisfied. Eve was always complaining and nagging. She bitched about not having enough.
So Atom would go out to work, in order to provide her with more and more.

Then she would complain that he wasn't spending enough time with her. He would stay home, and listen to her complain that she wasn't getting enough things. So he would go out and spend time attempting to acquire more fluffy stuffing. This whirlwind of confusion and contradiction was very frustrating for Atom. He didn't understand why she was throwing their love away.

When she wanted the camel, he never complained because he had to walk a mile to get it. He actually enjoyed the calming walk and the antics of a little blind wolf that appeared to be adopting him.

Sometimes Atom would work 18 to 20 hours a day, full moon to full moon on end. It was never enough. He wished Able would return from his quest, he needed help.

By the sweat of his brow, Atom worked to acquire the things that Eve **thought**, made her happy, or at least Quiet for a while. He had built up a stockpile that could last for a thousand life times, but it was never enough for who was slowly becoming disguised as Eve.

Atom and Eve were best friends and lovers at an earlier point in time and space. However, excitement and diamonds had become her new best friends as her heart became "Cold as Ice" She was willing to sacrifice their love.

Atom created a vast inventory of things for Eve. However, the more he produced, the more Bubba would sneak in and steal from him. Bubba figured that Atom wouldn't miss what he could embezzle from him…

The hidden 95% gratuity
Door # 18

Bubba was quite the showman. He figured that if he was going to industriously pursue this *pankration*[76] smack down with Atom he might as well dress for success! So he cloaked himself in an outlandish cape, a big funny looking hat, and assembled a staff of henchmen, groupies and hired… hands that were only seen on TV. He even acquired a new stage name and title.

He was the "Tax Man" – *Vicar*[77] of God. Why should he have to work when he could *flourish*[78] from the *prosperity*[79] of others?

Bubba was determined to win the game! His ego grew as it *parasitically*[80] fed on the fears of his relations. As his EGO swelled his body grew to enormous size. Who would dare challenge him? He had perfected the art of Emotional, Physical, and Spiritual Terrorism and would use tactics of disinformation to amasx an army to spew out his propaganda around the world. *Introspection*[81] would be *pilloried*[82] as the devils workshop. Geeze… talk about "little man" syndrome…

---

[76] Pankration: composed of two Greek words, "Pan" everything and "Kratos" meaning strength. Which considered to be interpreted as "Everything is allowed in strength; or 'All power' All strengths.

[77] Vicar: A substitute in office, a deputy or vicegerent. Hence, proxy; deputy; as, God's vicar. The priest of a parish the owner of the tithes of which is a layman (or formerly a spiritual corporation); any incumbent of a parish not a rector. An ecclesiastic who acts as a substitute for, or representative of another.

[78] Flourish: to be in a state of activity and production; expanding in influence, thriving; visibly doing well.

[79] Prosperity: Prosperous state or condition; successful progress; success. Prosper: to achieve economic success; succeeding at what one does.

[80] Parasitically: adv. Parasite: Gr. Antiq. One who eats at he table of another, repaying him with flattery. One of a class in religious rites who dinned with the priests after a sacrifice. A plant or animal living in, on, or with some other living organism (its host) at whose expense it obtains food, shelter, etc.

[81] Introspection: to practice self-examination.

[82] Pilloried: exposed to ridicule, public contempt, scorn or abuse.

Atom was working his ass off, the list of honey do's Eve assigned him was overwhelming, and so... he asked her to help him. He explained that with her assistance the project would only take a couple of hours, and they could spend the rest of the day together! This request was a bad idea, her response made him feel like a whipped pup.

She was infuriated that he had the audacity to make such a request. She stood up on her little soapbox and gave him a real tongue-lashing. To sum up this verbal thrashing, there was no way she was going to get her hands dirty, and she would kill him if he ever proposed any notion that may ever involve the possibility of another one of her fingernails breaking.

Guess what? ... That little chore that would have only taken a couple of hours or less if Eve helped; took many days for Atom to complete by himself, without any rest.
All the while, things kept disappearing...

When Atom returned home; tired, hungry, and very frustrated, Eve unloaded both barrels of bitch at him. She was irritated because he was gone so long, and still totally pissed off because he had asked her to help.

Able was still in the process of communicating with his Grandpa, and unavailable to assist his dad. Eve blamed Atom, for Able not blindly following her orders and the boy's exodus.

Eve began to bark her aggravation at Atom.
Bubba could have done it quicker!
Bubba would never ask me to get My hands dirty!
Bubba has servants to work for him so he doesn't have to! If you loved me, you would have made someone else do the work!
Bubba is so much smarter than you!
Bubba is the Dean of "La Vieille Ecole[83]."
You're such a dumb ass!" She screamed.

Ya Duh Ya Duh Ya Duh...

---

[83] La vieille école: French to English translation: The Old School. Metaphorically a.k.a. "the hard way."

Dear Tom…
Door # 19

Eves continual prattling about Bubba, finally put Atom to sleep.
While in his state of slumber, Eve ran away.

However she was courteous enough to leave a note. It contained these words:

"Atom, don't put funny ideas in your head. I do Love you. But I'm so young, I need to mature. I have to make my dreams come true. Just between you and me, I'm running away. Me and my El Camel. I can't stand it here. I've got to get away. Atom, please this is killing me. I do love you. Yet I still have to find what's missing. I need my answers. If I don't find them what will happen to me?
You call me a princess. This I'll never be. I lack the grace and charm. I always wanted to be one though.

I am not fit to wear your ring. Thus I'm returning it. I was proud to wear it, but I can no more wear such a thing than I could a crown. Forget it Atom, I'm not worth it. Don't get the idea that I'm feeling sorry for myself. Heck what is there to feel bad about? I'm a spoiled child, so I did a lot of thinking.
I thought about you, and then me, and what's separating us. It's only time. But what is time? The difference between today and yesterday This is time. What can time consume? Among the many things as dreams and reality is love.
Love is it the basis of all time? It is for me. And time spent with you is Love.
This is not a good-bye letter, I hope. I'll survive just fine on my own though.
I'm not making any mistakes with this one, Atom. You and I are perfect, but still how do I know there's nothing better? I will never know until I search. Only I don't want better. I only want you. I know in my heart that

60

you are the only man I could ever want to be married to. Yet still, again and again I must pursue my crazy pursuits, follow my ambitions, and live my dreams. So half and half, yes I will return to you some day way in the future, but first allow me the wonderful privilege of running around, trying everything new. Inviting fame and fortune in, flirting with disaster. Let me run like the wind, smile like the sun, see places, do things, meet people, dare myself to dream.

I can't spend all my life down at heel, sharing, giving, helping, serving good. Let me serve the devil awhile. I'd go crazy. Bless my soul.

You may not like this. You could even hate it. I just don't care to stay married and figure that I missed something right in the middle of everything. Like when I'm at that geriatric age of 30 or so, and take off to see what I missed.

I'm going to find a friend, a crowd first. Just to prove to myself that I didn't have to stay married to you, because you are my only friend. Allow me to make my mistakes before it's too late.

As for you, hell, you're still young. Young at heart. Go see what you can see. Just pray you come back. There's no hurry in anybody's life.

You and I really ought to practice being crazy at times. For if we can laugh through our life times together things may be a lot easier.

It's true. You and I do not laugh enough when we're together. Let alone when we're by ourselves. Don't let ghouling, sledding, playing football, tag, and baseball, skiing, telling jokes and getting drunk with your friends around a bonfire get old.

Atom dearest, we have become way too serious. And that scares me. Forgive me if this isn't what you wanted to hear. Yes, someday we'll be back together again. But for now we are just casual friends who need to laugh at the world.

I am deeply concerned about you, Sir Atom. Please be careful.

God bless you,

Eve

p.s. meet me on the dark side of the moon."

As it was in the beginning…

The Smoke Dog
Door # 20

Atom now faced the greatest challenge of his existence. He could find no reason to remain in this world. His heart was broken, and as he prepared to end his own life and send his spirit back home, a quiet voice asked him, 'who's going to take care of that little wolf?"

Atom had mastered many survival skills, however, once again he knew the difference between living and living well. The only threads that kept Atom clinging to life on this earth were the hope he found in the words Eve had written, and that special wolf that adopted him. It wasn't very clear who was the caretaker of whom. But the man and animal kept each other living for one reason or another.

When Atom slide into a state of depression, the little canine would use its mental telepathy, sending a quiet message to Atom, "Don't let the bastard win, don't let the bastard win."

Atom knew if he committed suicide, it would be a victory for this force of evil that had taken love away from the paradise that once existed. He knew that if he were to seek revenge, he would become a prisoner to his own anger.

Able finally returned home from his extended vision quest and found his Pop struggling to find a reason to remain here on earth. Atoms reason for being had abandoned him. Life after love was a fight for survival, and would prove to be one of the great tests of character.

Able shared his vision with his Pop. The man, who once was the boys' teacher, now became the student. Able helped his dad understand that there is nothing they can Do for Eve. The only thing Atom could do was just Be there for her, hold the sacred space, be compassionate and just keep sending her unconditional love. There will come a time when she will reconnect with her truth and will finally find what she went looking for. The world will begin to heal, when their souls begin the journey back to their future to a place of balanced inner peace.

Able asked about the story of this blind wolf[vi] that had been his dads' sidekick for a long time.
"Dad, Why does it keep following you around like it's your mini-mom?"

Atom told Able this old wolf is a very wise hero. Its wisdom came from its life experiences, and its knowledge flowed thru Creator. From birth this wolf knew that it had a life to live. A life no one else could live for it, a life to experience that no one could spare it from. This wolf was gifted with undeniable extra sensory perception because it could see from its heart.
She knows that if she was to deny or reject this connection, her survival in this world would be very difficult, and the cumulative stress of this dis-ease would take its toll.

This little one was born sightless. This blindness was not a handicap to this creature, but a precious gift. It learned that those with eyes had a limited view of life. They had eyes to see, however, they were constantly stepping and lying in their own poop. She was unable to observe this behavioral trait, but was gifted with the ability to avoid learning how to repeat it.

As a pup, this wolf was an outsider inside its own family. It made the choice to turn its back to her families patronizing prison and go away to survive on its own, rather than have her free will constantly cannibalized by her own families dependant need to be needed.
It had to do what it had to do, it wasn't easy, and the price she paid wasn't free. Leaving her family and loved ones behind was the hardest thing it thought there could ever be. She walked all the way through the fires and found that the terror that was real to previous generations no longer existed. The exaggerated imaginary fears were an inherited byproduct from a time long past. Those dinosaurs were gone, dead, extinct. And the grass definitely smelled and tasted greener outside the kennel.

For many years this special creature roamed the land. It journeyed from the beaches of the oceans to the tops of the highest mountains. She only nourished herself from those who would offer their life so she could live. Without any major effort on her part, everything she needed came to her.

There would be those who would attempt to prey on her, however, when they would look into her glazed over eyes, they could see a two tailed fish, the *vesica pisces*[84], the symbol of the intermediate realm between heaven and earth. They knew she was a sacred creature.

As this blind wolf was roaming about one winter day. Far off in the distance it could hear a pack of crying wolves. As she traveled closer, she recognized the howling songs of sadness. It was the horrified cries of her frightened family.
Her relatives were trapped in a blinding blizzard and at the brink of death.

Completely camouflaged by the blinding snowstorm, this little angel, made its way back to her pack. One grabbed her tail; another grabbed the tail of the first one, on and on. She was like an engine pulling a train forward to safety.

Her family was dumfounded when they discovered that this angel who had guided them to safety was… their family traitor.

Able suggested that they give this blind wolf a name, a handle with an appropriate reflection of its personality.

This canine *personified*[85] the *virtues*[86] of unconditional love. Atom suggested that the name must be a simple, yet mysterious riddle, for humans to decipher.

To protect the truth of its energetic identity, we shall call this little angel, DOG.
Her future generations will roam the land and serve mankind exemplifying the intrinsic value of unconditional love. These dogs will always be honest and true to themselves and others.

---

[84] Vesica Pices: Illustrated on the title page of this book.
[85] Personified: To conceive or represent. To be the personification of; to incarnate.
[86] Virtues: The ideal qualities in good human conduct.

They will show the humans doing unto others, how to BE.[vii]

Able replied, "dog! I don't understand?"

Atom said with a grin, "Son, do you remember the first time we went walking in the forest? I do. You probably didn't notice that you were under surveillance. You only looked in the direction we were traveling. You never looked back. I never mentioned what our destination was. Ya' didn't know where we were going, and ya didn't have a clue where you've been.
Do you remember how lost we were after our picnic lunch, when I told you to lead us back home?"

Able exclaimed, "Yeah Pop, I remember… I got real frustrated because we kept walking around in circles. That's the time I first met this wolf.
You told me to ask it to please show us the way home. And it Did!!"
"How did it do that, Pop?"
"Its simple son, it understands that it is being guided by someone up above. It isn't blinded by the illusion in front of its face."

"Huh?" Able replied with a confused questioning look on his face.
"Son, "Some can't see the forest because of the trees. However, because of the trees, this one knows there is a forest."

That sure was a long time ago, Pop. I learned the importance of looking back beyond my last step, so I could find my way back to where I began. Trails sure look different when you look at them in the opposite way. There were so many trees, I couldn't see my way out of the forest! I learned how to keep one eye on the future and one eye on the past so I could walk a straight line home, not in circles.

I wish Mom's crazy cat would learn that lesson. It keeps orbiting around the tree we have it leashed to until the rope gets too sort and it whines because it is choking itself. It keeps trying to go the same way. It's too stupid to unwind.

Now I understand! Read the word dog backwards and it spells unconditional love! There is a lot to be said about looking at stuff form another perspective.

That's why it took so long for me to read Grandfathers airmail. Just between you and me Dad, Pop's handwriting font sucks.

But if all her ancestors will be known as dogs, we need to give her a personal name. She's so special. Can we do that?"

So they thought about it for a while as they were looking at the granite stones all around them, and thought of her story.

Her story wasn't as clearly noticeable as these big rocky boulders. The theme of her life story was a common oversight. It was more like that of a drop of ocean water, much smaller, yet contains the entire essence of the greater. Just like Atoms name.

So Able gave this little spiritual warrior, this dog, the perfect name... Pebbles.

It was time for them to move on, not only for that day, but also for the journey through many entangled lifetimes. As Atom sat beside his only son, he passed on some words his mom told him when he was young.

Able listened closely to what he said.

... Be a "Simple Kind of Man"; don't forget there is someone up above. Forget your lust for rich mans gold; all that you need is in your soul...Kola, if you do it this way, I will be with you and we can help our grandchildren some day...

As they took their first steps toward their futures, Able stepped in a squishy pile of Pebbles poop. Able looked at his Pop who was grinning from ear to ear. With one voice, father and son together yelled, "Shit Happens!"

Pebbles celebrated her amusement with these boys. She began chasing her tail. She was spinning around with an excited Taz-spastic furry that accelerated to a warped speed of fiery light. The sound that resonated from this tornado howled a loony tune.

When she stopped, the dirt and dust in the air cleared, the soot settled, and the coat she was wearing appeared to be...Smokey.

And the tail wagged the goofy Smokey dog.

Like father...Like son
Door # 21

Eve's second child was born into the world. He had a very different personality than Able. He was exceedingly demanding, and obsessed with control. A big stick was what he carried instead of a security blanket. He was named Cane.

When Able was conceived, he was conceived with the emotion of Love. Able was the re-incarnate emotional body of his parents.

Cane was conceived under different circumstances. However, he also was the re-incarnate emotional body of His parents at the time of his conception. Cane *emulated*[87] his father's ungodly performance. Cane would sing their party line theme song as the father and son rocked and rolled through the time bands on their "Highway to Hell."

...No stop signs, speed limit
No body's gonna slow me down
Like a wheel, gonna spin it
Nobody's gonna mess me around...

Bubba's sister got a gig in a corresponding cable network as the seducer of men. This operative merger would prove to be highly profitable. Their backers would reap some pretty good dividends as the success of the 'in-co-operation' expanded.

---

[87] Emulate: To strive to equal or excel (another); rivalry. Emulation: Ambition or endeavor to equal or excel.

ReBoot?
Door # 22

Atom and Eve would continue through the divine sequence of events that we all go through on this earth. They would never feel safe riding the bi-cycle of karma on their circles of lifetimes, as long as they adhered to the Old School energy curriculum. The antique duality energy theory of opposing forces that perpetually creates the dramatic struggles and traumatic conflicts within our lives.

Eve would persist with her ongoing search for what was missing. She would continue to pursue her crazy pursuits, follow her ambitions, and live her dreams. She enjoyed the privilege of running around, trying everything new. She invited in fame and fortune, flirted with disaster and even served the devil at times.

Her shopping spree for something better would revolve through many lifetimes. She would acquire and pay off enormous karmic depts. The wealth of experience she gained in her many adventures would lead to a richness of life, which for the many who refused to see the external ripple effect of her inner turmoil - would become a focal point of envy.

There would be many life events that would change gears and allow these two souls to touch, and then go their separate ways.
For Atom these would be the highest of highs when they were together. Her smile would light up his life. Then he would roller coaster down to the lowest of lows when she would run away again. He got to experience the old adage, 'hell hath no furry like a woman scorned!' Why did he have to leave her to go on this trip? There were life-times when the Eve's made him wish he never left home.

In the pursuit to keep his promise, Atom would encounter many challenging contradicting dead-end roadblocks as he muddled his way through the maze's of life. He faced difficulty with understanding how Eve couldn't be honest with the love she once knew in her heart, and at the same time continue being honest with herself by trying to prove something to herself by running away from what she was looking for.

In Atom's mind, Eve's balancing act of this repetitive imbalanced behavior was not logical. This frustrated him to no end. Until he discovered that the imbalance in her was a reflection of some imbalance within him. It was time for Atom to quit playing Bubba's game, and realign and attune with his spiritual self and move toward a new balanced consciousness. Even if it meant that he had to leave his family and loved ones behind.

Atom finally understood the message his Pop sent to him through his son Able.
Compassion. He had to have compassion for himself and everyone. He had to stop trying to change the world, but rather to honor each and every individual for their choices and their journey. It would take great compassion and strength of character for Atom to allow Eve the wonderful privilege of experiencing the lives she chose even if those lives appear to be leading the world toward a catastrophic train wreck. It requires an extreme understanding of compassion to unconditionally love, and forgive those who continue to choose to live in the addictions. Maybe that's why sometimes it's called tough love. In another time frame he phrased it this way; "I see what I see. And it hurts because of what I've seen." In other words… been there before.

Atom immediately experienced an unexpected twist. He wondered that maybe, just maybe, he discovered something… Something he was looking for, even though he didn't know what he was looking for. At that moment an uncomfortable shivering chill went through his spine, because; he realized he had been 'shopping.' But that was just a scary side effect of this probable breakthrough.

As he put the pieces together he thought maybe he and Eve were put here to push and pull each other, dancing through a mountain of fertilizer in the vortex of evil to discover a potential within themselves that only the other could see or feel.

Had they been in a tangled tango with and without each other to resurrect something that they either didn't know existed, overlooked because it was too simple, or repressed for a desire to prove something, self imposed limitation, promise, or another?

Maybe the tail he was chasing was his tale. But he couldn't have discovered this phenomenon without chasing her... *phat*[88]'tail'! ☯

But the funny thing was, anytime one of these two kids would illuminate a piece of the others loving light, the other would say, "No that's not it!" And run away from their own-mirrored reflection.
Sunlight isn't harmful to soul stealing vampires; it's the light of truth and unconditional LOVE that makes them recoil.

Suddenly, Atom realized that he had been fighting his dancing lessons all along.

"Life's a Dance." "You learn as you go. Sometimes you lead, sometimes you follow." And, sometimes you get drugged around to what you are connected to. Atom could feel the burdening weight of his responsibility for Eve and the world, lifting from his shoulders. He no longer worried about what he didn't know. And he finally understood what his Pop's meant when he said "failure isn't failure if a lesson from it's learned."

Atom prayed at his altar of consciousness for the day that Eve's special wolf would find her.
He prayed that she would look in her soul and find the balance of serenity, courage, and wisdom she went shopping for.

"It's a wonderful life" What a great show!

"The angels have waited for so long" to see if the long shot they wagered on eons ago... will take place.

---

[88] Phat: *Slang* Excellent; first-rate: phat fashion. [Earlier, sexy (said of a woman), of unknown orig.]

The stages are set. The bands are playing. The new color "frequency" films continue to twist and turn.

Here we are! In the NOW,
Occupying a meridian point on many integrated arteries and veins of time.
Just peeking into a great mystery of how this little high school science project possibly became the *modem*[89] for the largest Universe City - Internet / Web -TV /spiritually interactive virtual reality, star gate hollow-deck dramatic traumatic sit-com show- me sporting game show... EVER!

So welcome;
Welcome to the "Grand Illusion"
Take a step up to see what's happened.
You paid the price, time to get a clear view of your show.
The angels still bet. The bands are still playing.
Start your heart to feel it pounding.
Still afraid to seek the truth of who you are?

You've been fooled by the radio, TV, and the magazines...
They sell you photographs of how your life should be...
But that's just someone else's plan you see.
So if you think this story is complete delusion, because you love to play the games.
Just remember its Hue-man Confusion
There's no one but you to blame
It's a karma game...
We're all the same...

So if you think your life is complete confusion because the neighbor laid your babe.
Just remember that it's a grand illusion. Deep inside we're all the same.
On this earth its competition; sign right up with blind ambition
Get yourself a new El Camel.

---

[89] Modem: A device that converts data for transmission, as by telephone, to data processing equipment

71

T.G. Maier

Someday soon you'll stop to ponder why on earth's who's hell you're under
You made the grade and still you wonder why that you are…
…in a material world
…in a material world
…in a material world

That little antique dog on the cover…Pebbles…was my blind wolf. But that's another story.

What if…
The Future IS the Past Healed?
Mitakuye Oyasin[90]

---

[90] Mitakuye Oyasin: Lakota language: we are all related; all my relatives; all are related

Lets' Make a Deal Door…?

It's your mind…
<u>Suffering is optional!</u>

It's your choice…

18 Things we can learn from a Dog.

1.   Never pass up the opportunity to go for a Joy ride.

2.   Allow the experience of fresh air and the wind in your face to be pure ecstasy.

3.   When loved ones come home, always run to greet them.

4.   When it's in your best interest, practice obedience.

5.   Let others know when they have invaded your territory.

6.   Take naps, and stretch before rising.

7.   Run, romp, and play daily.

8.   Eat with gusto and enthusiasm.

9.   BE LOYAL

10.   Never pretend to be something you're not.

11.   If what you want is buried, dig until you find it.

12.   When someone is having a bad day, be silent, sit close by, and nuzzle him or her gently.

13.   Thrive on attention and let people touch you.

14.   Avoid biting when a simple growl will do.

15.   On hot days, drink lots of water and lie under a shady tree.

16.   When you're happy, dance around and wag your entire body.

17.   Delight in the simple joy of a long walk.

18.   No matter how often you're scolded, don't buy into that guilt thing and put... run right back and make friends.
-unknown

REFERENCES

Vibrational Medicine, Richard Gerber, M.D.
(Bear & Company, 2001) ISBN: 1-879181-58-4

The Massage Connection: Anatomy, Physiology & Pathology, Dr. Kalyani Premkumar, MBBS MD MSc(Med Ed) RMT
(VanPub Books, 1997) ISBN: 0-9680730-1-8

The Polarity Process, Franklyn Sills.
(North Atlantic Books, 1989, 2002) ISBN: 1-55643-410-3

Far Walker, Larry Leonard.
(Breitenbush Books, 1988) ISBN: 0-932576-60-5

Animal-Speak, Ted Andrews
(Llewellyn Publications, 1993) ISBN: 0-87542-028-1

Conversations with God, an uncommon dialogue. Book 1. Neale Donald Walsh
(Hampton Roads, 1995) ISBN: 0399142789
Conversations with God, an uncommon dialogue. Book 2. Neale Donald Walsh
(Hampton Roads, 1997) ISBN: 1-5714-056-2
Conversations with God, an uncommon dialogue. Book 3. Neale Donald Walsh
(Hampton Roads, 1998) ISBN: 1-57174-103-8
The Little Soul and the Sun, Neale Donald Walsh
(Hampton Roads, 1998) ISBN: 1-57174-087-2

Virus of the Mind, Richard Brodie
(Integral Press, 1996) ISBN: 0-963001-1-7

The Seat of the Soul, Gary Zukav
(Simon & Schuster, 1989) ISBN: 0-671-69507-X

The Dancing Wu Li Masters, Gary Zukav
(Bantam Books, 1979) ISBN: 0-553-26382-X

Soul Retrieval, Mending the Fragmented Self, Sandra Ingerman.
(HarperSanFrancisco, 1991) ISBN: 0-06-250406-1

Mother Earth Spirituality, Ed McGaa.
(HarperSanFrancisco, 1990) ISBN: 0-06-250596-3

Native Wisdom, Ed McGaa.
(Four Directions Publishing, 1995) ISBN: 0-9645173-1-0

Soul Mates, Thomas Moore.
(Harper Perennial, 1994) ISBN: 0-06-092575-2

Many Lives Many Masters, Brian L. Weiss, M.D.
(A Fireside Book, Simon & Schuster, 1988) ISBN: 0-671-65786-0

Webster's New Collegiate Dictionary,
(G.& C. Merriam Co. 1961)

The American Heritage College Dictionary, Fourth edition
(Houghton Mifflin Company 2002)

The Way to Happiness, L. Ron Hubbard
(Bridge Publications, 1989) ISBN: 0-88404-809-8

Pangaea, USGS [This Dynamic Earth, USGS]
URL: http://pubs.usgs.gov/publications/text/historical.html

Movies:

It's a Wonderful Life, Directed by Frank Capra, 1946.
Staring: James Stewart and Donna Reed.

Frequency, New Line Productions 2001
Staring: Dennis Quaid and Jim Caviezel

The Matrix, Warner Bros. 1999
Staring: Keanu Reeves and Laurence Fishburne

About the Author

With a career that has covered a quarter of a century as a bricklayer, T.G. Maier has acquired many skills required to assemble big puzzles. At the age of 40 he began looking at life from a spiritual perspective. On the return home from a summer long road trip with his 16 year old dog, Pebbles, he asked why certain life events happened. He was told that it was up to him to put the parts he receives on the road of life together. This story twisted out of the photos and introspective journaling's of the adventures with that little antique dog and her human. Mr. Maier lives in Kansas City, Missouri, and moonlights as a certified massage therapist.

End notes

[i] Vibrational Medicine, Richard Gerber

[ii] The Little Soul and the Sun – Neil Donald Walsh

[iii] Comic strip NON-SEQUITOR Wiley 1999 "The real reason Satin was banished from Heaven"

[iv] W.A.R. We Are Right – unknown comic strip.

[v] Synergistic Energy eXchange (s.e.x.) Conversations With God – Neil Donald Walsh

[vi] Story of the Blind Wolf, from the book "Farwalker" by Larry Leonard

[vii] 18 things you can learn from a dog.

Printed in the United States
24287LVS00003B/220-297